BIRDS—RIGHT BEFORE YOUR EYES

Written and Illustrated
by
John R. Wiessinger

Foreword by Les Line,
Editor, *Audubon* magazine

ENSLOW PUBLISHERS, INC.

Bloy St. & Ramsey Ave.
Box 777
Hillside, N. J. 07205
U.S.A.

P.O. Box 38
Aldershot
Hants GU12 6BP
U.K.

Library of Congress Cataloging-in-Publication Data

Wiessinger, John R.
    Birds-right before your eyes / written and illustrated by John R.
Wiessinger : foreword by Les Line.
       p. cm. — (Right before your eyes)
    Includes index.
    Summary: Presents detailed drawings of American birds with
information on their biology and behavior.
    ISBN 0-89490-167-2
    1. Birds. [1. Birds.] I. Title.
  II. Series: Right before your eyes (Hillside, N.J.)
  QL673.W536 1988

                                87-27278
                                    CIP
                                      AC

Printed in the United States of America

10 9 8 7 6 5 4 3 2 1

CONTENTS

Foreword   5
Introduction   6

I. WHO'S WHO

Animals All   7
Birds of a Feather   8
To Each His Own   9
Domestic Life   10
Mistaken Identity   11
Just A Sparrow   12
Ups and Downs   13
Seeing Red   14
Landlubber   15

II. HOW THINGS WORK

Solo Duet   16
Lube Job   17
Goosebumps   18
Cold Duck on Ice!   19
Asleep on the Job!   20
Flight Goggles   21
These Eyes Have It!   22
Now You See It. . .   23
Optical Illusion   24

III. ON THE MOVE

The Sky's the Limit   25
Thumbs Up   26
Dark or Light?   27
Staying on Top   28
Why Go?   29
Getting Ready   30
Night Flight   31
Pass It On   32
Squatter's Rights   33

IV. HUNTING AND HIDING

Search Image   34
Screams in the Night   35
Silent Night   36
Fitting the Bill   37
Look Before You Eat   38
Looking or Listening?   39
Headlines   40
Look Again   41
Blending is Better   42

V. FAMILY MATTERS

Turkey on Display   43
Serious Business   44
Early Bird   45
Over Easy   46
Jail Break   47
Take Your Pick   48
Foster Care   49
That's Hard to Swallow!   50
Disposable Diapers   51

VI. BIRDS AND PEOPLE

Bird *vs.* Bonnet   52
Alien Invasion   53
To the Rescue?   54
Flying Cigars   55
Helping the Horde   56
O Christmas Tree   57
Sharing   58
A Success Story?   59
Why Care?   60

Index   61

FOREWORD

A flowering dogwood tree thrives right next to the railroad station where commuters from the Hudson River village in which I live wait each weekday morning for the train to New York City. Adorned with creamy white flowers in spring and fire-engine red berries in autumn, that tree is the stage, all year long, for one of the most remarkable vocalists in the kingdom of birds. Even lawyers and stockbrokers have been known to lift their eyes from *The Wall Street Journal* and smile in wonderment when this feathered Pavarotti breaks into song.

It's not that his voice is sweet. It certainly can be. Or it may squeak like a rusty gate. What is so remarkable is his repertoire. It includes the songs of two or three dozen other birds, imitated so perfectly that they fool not only the ears of expert bird-listeners but electronic analysis, too. And it imitates not just birds, but also frogs, crickets, and barking dogs—plus the whistle of the rushing express train on the middle track!

Our singer has an appropriate name. *The mockingbird.* Indians called him "four hundred tongues," and he is a real gee-whiz bird, whose story is bound to fascinate even people who tell you that birds are boring. Audubon painted mockingbirds fearlessly attacking a rattlesnake to defend their nest, and he wasn't exaggerating.

But there is a bit of gee-whiz in every bird, even the commonest sparrow. John Wiessinger knows that, and he relates some of those wondrous facts with neat drawings and fun-to-read descriptions. He has given us a book that will spark the interest of a new generation of birdwatchers, while reminding us oldtimers of the things that got us hooked on birds so many years ago.

Les Line

Editor
Audubon magazine

5

INTRODUCTION

Birds are fun! Since ancient time, their songs have delighted us, their feathers and flight have fascinated us, their habits have intrigued us. Almost anywhere you go, from ocean to desert, from the tropics to the arctic, you'll find birds. And birdwatchers. More than any other animal science, ornithology (the study of birds) appeals to the nonscientist.

Each of our more than 650 North American species has its own special story. But there is more to bird study than just identifying a species or a song. There are endless questions about birds: How do birds sleep on a perch without falling off? How do they find enough food for their active bodies? Why don't their feet freeze in winter? How can they migrate for thousands of miles and return to a specific yard?

Fortunately, we don't have to look far afield for either the questions or the fascinating answers. Too often, people have looked to the exotic birds for interesting information—ostriches, penguins, peacocks. But the birds that surround us, that "rub elbows" with us all the time, are every bit as deserving of our attention. And every time we see them, we are reminded of what we have learned. How satisfying to learn why Blue Jays look blue to us—and to prove it to ourselves with a Blue Jay feather from the sidewalk. Even the most drab backyard sparrow takes on a new life for us when we learn something about it.

Nature cannot be studied like a novel with a beginning, a middle, and an end. It is a vast assortment of bits of information. But as you learn more, those bits gradually come together to form a larger picture. The facts in this book are presented in the same way. Every page stands on its own; you can read the book back to front, middle to end, or hit-or-miss. But I hope that as you read, you'll gain a new respect for and enjoyment of the birds that are your neighbors. No need to look to the far corners of the earth. There is more than enough to fill a thousand books, just about the birds *right before your eyes.*

Animals All

The term <u>animal</u> is regularly used to distinguish <u>mammals</u> (creatures which nurse their young) from birds, frogs, worms and so on. All mammals are animals, but not all animals are mammals! This confusion of terms has led many people to think of organisms such as birds and frogs as something other than animals.

All of the organisms shown here are ANIMALS, even though they are not mammals!

Birds of a Feather

Quick! What makes a bird a bird?
What does it have that no other
animal has?

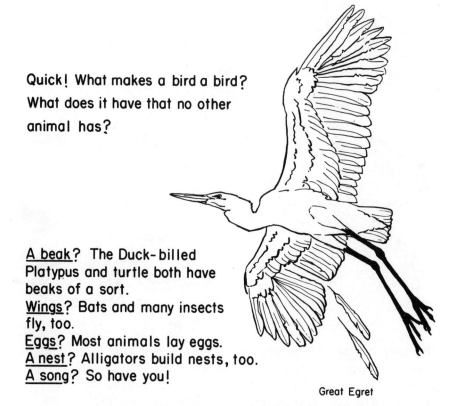

<u>A beak</u>? The Duck-billed
Platypus and turtle both have
beaks of a sort.
<u>Wings</u>? Bats and many insects
fly, too.
<u>Eggs</u>? Most animals lay eggs.
<u>A nest</u>? Alligators build nests, too.
<u>A song</u>? So have you!

Great Egret

But <u>all</u> birds — and <u>only</u> birds — have feathers. It's as
simple as that.

8

To Each His Own

An animal's "niche" (rhymes with stitch) is its occupation within the environment. No two species can ever occupy exactly the same niche. However, the difference may be as subtle as the parts of a tree on which two warbler species forage for insects.

A more obvious niche distinction is that between the Red-tailed Hawk and the Great Horned Owl. They are about the same size; both feed on small mammals, birds, and reptiles; both hunt on the wing; and both inhabit a wide variety of habitats across almost all of North America.

The biggest difference in their niches?
One works the night shift.

Domestic Life

Domestic animals have traded self-reliance for safety. Most have been selectively bred for specific needs (like food, work or fur) and are often very different from their ancestors.

Camouflage and defense mechanisms are not essential in domestic animals, so we have been able to breed white mice, delicate racing horses, hornless sheep, tiny dogs, and so on.

Wild Mallard   Domestic Duck

Ducks were originally domesticated by the Romans. Most barnyard varieties are derived from the wild Mallard. The heavier, larger domestic doesn't fly well (and doesn't need to), but it gives us more meat than its wild counterpart.

Mistaken Identity

Herons are often mistaken for cranes. Although these two groups may look alike, they are not closely related.

Most herons have an obvious "kink" in their necks, and after takeoff they fly with their necks folded in an **S**.

Great Blue Heron

Sandhill Crane

Only two species of cranes are found in North America: the endangered Whooping Crane and the Sandhill Crane. Both fly with outstretched neck and are uncommon almost everywhere.

Just A Sparrow

To many people, sparrows are uninteresting, unwelcome, introduced pests. Often confused with the House Sparrow from Europe (a weaver bird, not a true sparrow), sparrows live in many different habitats and many add beautiful songs to the outdoors.

Chipping Sparrow

There are more than 30 species of sparrows in North America. Because their colors are subdued browns and grays, we often miss the rich variations in their plumage patterns. Many species frequent bird feeders, giving people a chance to become better acquainted with these interesting birds.

Song Sparrow

The next time you see a small, brown bird, don't say "it's just a sparrow"; look closely and see if you can identify it.

White-throated Sparrow

12

Ups and Downs

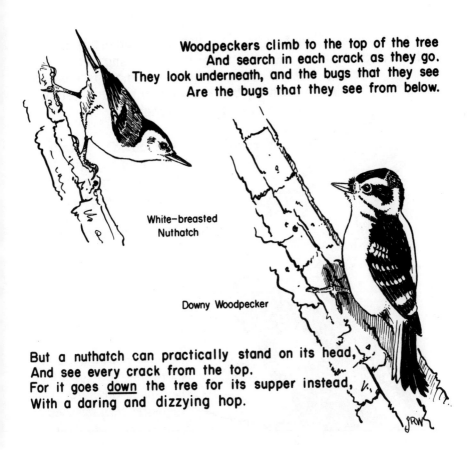

Woodpeckers climb to the top of the tree
And search in each crack as they go.
They look underneath, and the bugs that they see
Are the bugs that they see from below.

White—breasted
Nuthatch

Downy Woodpecker

But a nuthatch can practically stand on its head,
And see every crack from the top.
For it goes <u>down</u> the tree for its supper instead,
With a daring and dizzying hop.

The nuthatch is easy to tell from its friends,
A grey—black—and—white feathered clown:
While other birds busy themselves going <u>up,</u>
The nuthatch is on its way <u>down</u>.

Seeing Red

The Red-winged Blackbird may be the most numerous land bird in North America. Each spring it is seen and heard across most of the continent. The male is easy to identify with its black body and red and yellow "epaulets" (shoulder patches).

The colorful patches do NOT attract females, but are used to intimidate rival males seeking a territory. Suitable wetland territories are limited, so only some of the males mate successfully.

female

Red-winged
Blackbird

male
displaying

Female Redwings look more like sparrows than blackbirds and are regularly misidentified. Ever wonder why you never saw the females before? They're out there; they are just not as obvious!

Landlubber

When we think of shorebirds, like sandpipers and plovers, of course we think of them living near water. But the Killdeer (a plover) is the best known and most widespread North American shorebird and often nests far from water — in plowed fields, dry uplands, pastures, and even lawns.

Killdeer

A Killdeer nest is nothing more than a "scrape," or slight depression, often in a gravelly area, but its small, speckled eggs are well camouflaged even though fully exposed. Killdeer are probably best known for their loud, aerial, *Kill-Dee* cry which they begin at the slightest disturbance.

Solo Duet

A mere sparrow can out-sing an opera star! Human vocal cords are in the larynx: one set of cords, one note at a time. A bird uses a special organ called the syrinx (SEER-inks), located where the two bronchi join. The double structures of the syrinx (named for the Pipes of Pan) allow the bird to sing two distinct notes at the same time — a duet with itself.

J.WIESSINGER

The Wood Thrush has one of the most beautiful songs of local birds. A timid species, its woodland voice is seldom heard at close range...... but it is a voice Pavarotti would admire.

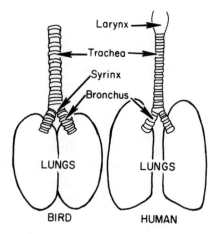

Larynx

Trachea

Syrinx

Bronchus

LUNGS   LUNGS

BIRD   HUMAN

Lube Job

Daily feather maintenance is not a matter of looks, but of health. Most birds have an oil-producing preen gland above the base of the tail. A bird periodically nibbles or rubs the gland, getting the oil on its beak and head. Subsequent preening spreads the oil over feathers, legs and feet.

Redhead Ducks preening

The oil probably has several uses. It improves the insulating and water repellent properties of the feathers, seems to keep bills and legs healthy, and may even help some birds produce vitamin D from sunshine.

A bird's feathers are its roof, transportation, and blanket. No wonder preening receives such high priority.

Goosebumps

Everyone gets goosebumps. Ever wonder why?

Mourning Dove

Tiny muscles in the skin of mammals and birds contract, pulling on the base of each hair or feather, when the animal is cold or excited. This mechanism, which fluffs out hair and feathers, traps extra air next to the skin and helps insulate the animal against the cold (or makes it look bigger to an enemy!). On an especially cold day mammals and birds look fatter. They haven't gained any weight; they are just trying to keep warm.

Cottontail

Humans have these same muscles. But with our skimpy "fur," goosebumps don't do us much good!

Cold Duck On Ice !

How can a duck stand all day in icy water or snow without suffering frostbite ?

MALLARD DUCKS

Many aquatic birds have a special network of directly connecting arteries and veins in their lower legs which bypasses the capillaries. This network permits the warm, outflowing arterial blood to mix with and warm the colder returning venous blood in the foot. The duck's foot stays warm enough to avoid freezing yet cool enough to avoid the loss of too much body heat.

Asleep on the Job !

HOW DOES A BIRD MANAGE TO STAY ON A BRANCH WHILE IT SLEEPS ? IT'S AUTOMATIC !

The muscles which cause a bird's leg to bend are attached to the toes by tendons which stretch over the ankle. When these muscles contract or when the bird squats, the tendons pull on the base of the toes, causing the toes to curl.

American Robin

Thigh

Knee

Leg (drumstick)

Ankle

Tendon

The more the bird bends its ankle, the tighter the curl. When a bird sleeps, its ankle is bent to its maxi- mum and the toes grip the perch with surprising strength.

Flight Goggles

Birds have a "third eyelid," called the nictitating (NICK-tih-TATE-ing) membrane. This transparent membrane can wipe across the cornea to clean and moisten it without requiring that the eye blink. Many scientists believe that while in flight, birds keep this membrane over the eye to reduce the drying effects of the air stream—— built-in goggles!

Barn Swallow

Amphibians, reptiles, birds and mammals all have this membrane but not all are functional. In humans, it is reduced to that small bump in the inner corner of your eye.

nictitating membrane (white)
partially covering eye

Laughing Gull

These Eyes Have It !

Although the world is filled with color for us, some animals see it only in shades of gray. Birds, turtles, fish, primates, and some lizards are the only vertebrates (animals with backbones) which we know can see color. Most mammals cannot.

Box Turtle

Cardinal

The fisherman who changes from one color lure to another may be making a wise move after all; the debate over whether fish can really see colors has been settled. On the other hand, the hunter who wears International Orange to protect himself from other humans is merely gray to the deer he hunts.

Skink

Bass

Now You See It......

The iridescent throat patch, or gorget (GOR-jet), of a male Ruby-throated Hummingbird doesn't always show. The gorget's beautiful flash of color is highly directional and shows only when the viewer is between the bird and the sun. The brilliant color is due to the way light is scattered by a special feather structure; the feathers' <u>real</u> color is a dark gray.

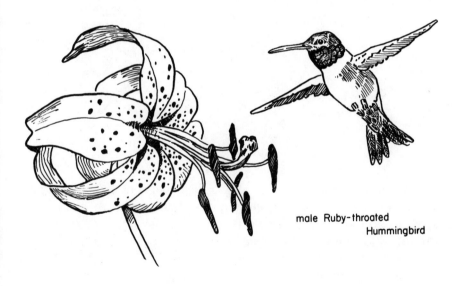

male Ruby-throated
Hummingbird

It takes only a small movement of the male's head and his flash of color completely disappears. Look quickly. Now you see it........now you don't!

Optical Illusion

That Blue Jay at your feeder isn't blue at all; it's a dull brownish gray!

BLUEJAY

JRW

The color you see is not   blue pigment but the result of a thin layer of cells overlying the feathers' true color. The special structure of these cells allows most light through but reflects blue light waves. The vivid blue color is visible as long as a feather's microscopic structure remains intact. If a Blue Jay feather is crushed, damaging its construction, the "true" color will show.

As far as we know, there are no "true blue" birds. They all rely on structural blue.

The Sky's the Limit

One of the most obvious questions about birds is how fast they can fly! Most birds cruise at speeds from 20-50 miles per hour but can travel much faster for short distances. Recording their <u>maximum</u> speeds isn't easy.

Dunlin

For the record, the Dunlin, a small sandpiper, has been clocked at 110 mph or more in level, flapping flight. Although the Peregrine Falcon has been credited with diving speeds of 175–200 mph, experimenters have not been able to document it at more than about 80 mph. Off the record, the fastest North American bird in flapping flight appears to be the little White-throated Swift —— which has been estimated at 200 mph!

Thumbs Up

We take air travel for granted, but the complexities of bird flight are still under study.

alula

Red-shouldered Hawk

Birds have a group of short feathers, called the alula (AL-u-la), on each thumb. These small feathers appear to be very important. At slow speeds, like take-off and landing, a bird may "stall" without additional lift. Today's jets have the same problem. Jets use their front wing flaps to provide that extra lift. Scientists think that birds came up with the same solution millions of years ago—— the alula.

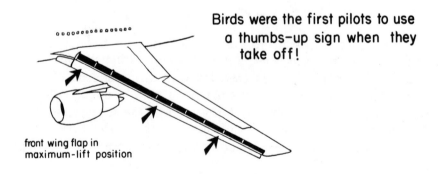

front wing flap in
maximum-lift position

Birds were the first pilots to use a thumbs-up sign when they take off!

Dark or Light?

Do you prefer dark meat or light?
Ever wondered why you have a choice?

Birds like pheasants, quail, grouse, turkeys, and chickens have two kinds of muscles, dark and light. The white (breast) muscles provide powerful bursts of flight but tire quickly. The dark meat (legs), by contrast, provides sustained activity. It's no wonder that a pheasant would rather run than fly. Birds which migrate or make sustained flights, like ducks, hawks, crows and robins, don't have white meat. Theirs is all dark——not as powerful, perhaps, but built for the long haul.

Ring-necked Pheasant

Staying on Top

With the approach of winter each year, most members of the grouse family begin growing "snowshoes." Tiny scaly projections grow out from the sides of each toe, greatly increasing the surface area of their feet. Just like the snowshoes people wear, the increased surface area distributes the weight of the bird over a greater area, and the grouse doesn't sink as deeply into the snow. For a bird which does a lot of walking to find food, staying on top of the snow is an important adaptation to life in the North Woods.

Ruffed Grouse

scaly projections on
Ruffed Grouse toes in winter

Why Go?

Why do so many birds fly north each spring when they could remain south where it's warm and avoid the dangers and stress of migration?

There is no simple answer; there seem to be a variety of reasons. The greater availability of food in the north in the summer coupled with longer days in which to forage for their young are probably two of the main reasons.

In any case, there must be considerable advantage to migration; millions do so every year! Birds often return to the very spot where they lived the previous summer.

Getting Ready

It may seem that migration is caused by a food shortage, that hunger pushes birds south in search of something to eat each fall. Actually, migratory birds begin preparing for migration well before any food shortage or bad weather occurs.

Northern (Baltimore) Oriole

Decreasing daylength probably signals the time to "get ready." Well before leaving, birds eat extra food and store large amounts of fat in their bodies to provide fuel for their journey. Once a bird is physically prepared for migration, temperature, food abundance, weather, and other reasons can trigger the actual time it leaves.

Night Flight

Large numbers of migrants travel to their winter or summer quarters at night rather than during the day. Navigation at night presents a variety of problems but several navigational aids are known to guide birds on their journey.

1. Sunset glow helps the birds "set" their navigational direction as they start out.
2. Stars provide clear-night navigational aids.
3. The earth's magnetic field is used as a compass.

These are <u>some</u> of the <u>known</u> methods of navigation; there are no simple answers. Each bird probably has a variety of methods available to it. If one method is blocked (as on a cloudy night), the bird can switch to another.

Pass It On

Migration is an energy-draining task. Any help a bird can get during migration increases its chances for survival.

Birds such as geese have evolved a method which is believed to improve migratory efficiency — they fly in **V** formation.

In flight, each bird loses some air over its wings, which causes an upswelling vortex of air behind it known as a slipstream. In a V formation, each bird (except the leader) flies aside and above the bird in front, resting its inner wingtip over the rising vortex of air lost from the bird ahead. The energy lost from one bird's wing is probably "passed along" and used by the next bird in line.

Canada Geese

Studies indicate that this method may actually improve the range of formation-flying birds by more than 50%.

Squatter's Rights

Each fall many bird species migrate, others do not. The American Robin, however, is a partial migrant; individual Robins may or may not fly south.

Robins which do remain in cold climates can improve the insulation of their feathers by fluffing them up to trap air. Since a great deal of energy is needed to fuel a bird's body, a bird's greatest danger is not freezing —— but starving !

American Robin

Why should a Robin put up with winter temperatures when it could go south? The hardy ones who last the winter have squatter's rights to the best nesting sites in the spring.

Search Image

How an animal looks for food can have a marked effect upon how much it finds.

Forming a **search image** — a "picture in its mind" of what it is looking for — can increase an animal's feeding success. Once it has a search image for a specific abundant food (a certain kind of caterpillar, for example) it looks only for that, ignoring most other foods. It has only one food to hunt for, and when that food is found, it doesn't have to decide whether it's edible or not, so the animal has fewer decisions to make. This improves the speed with which it finds and captures food.

Warbler

Screams in the Night

Eerie screams in the night may mean ghosts or goblins — or just a Barn Owl. Despite the Barn Owl's hair-raising scream, it is actually harmless and even beneficial to humans. It often roosts in barns, and its diet of small mammals like mice makes it particularly helpful to farmers.

Barn Owl

The Barn Owl's acute night vision helps it locate food. But even in total darkness, the owl can still home in on the slightest noise. Its dish-shaped face may act like a TV satellite disc to help collect and focus sound. Owls fly silently, so prey are often captured before they know danger is near.

Silent Night

Owls have keen hearing and eyesight to help them find their prey on a dark night. But locating an animal is only the first step; the owl must be able to take it by surprise.

Most birds are noisy in flight, but not owls. The outer feather on each wing has serrations on its leading (front) edge which reduce air disturbance and noise from the wing. Finely fringed edges on the trailing portion of the flight feathers further reduce noise, making silent flight possible.

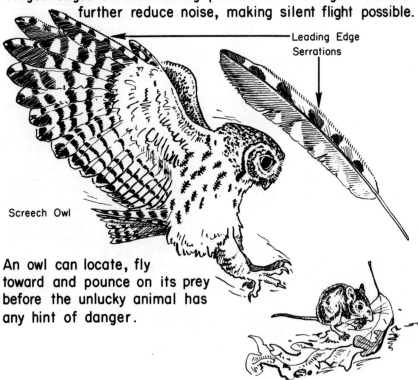

Leading Edge Serrations

Screech Owl

An owl can locate, fly toward and pounce on its prey before the unlucky animal has any hint of danger.

Fitting the Bill

Teeth are heavy equipment to try and fly with. Birds get by with lightweight bills, or beaks, custom-made to suit a given bird's diet. A bird's bill says a lot about its diet.

Herons: long neck and bill are a spring-loaded spear.

Many ducks: sieve-like bill edge strains out water plants & animals.

Warblers: precision tool picks small insects off trees.

Woodpeckers: hard, sharp chisel mounted on extra-thick skull.

Hummingbirds: long thin tube dips deep into flowers for nectar.

Hawks: strongly hooked bill tears prey apart.

Finches: seedeaters are equipped with a nutcracker.

Look Before You Eat

Ducks look something like Donald and dabble on the surface for tiny bits of food, right? Not always.

Mergansers <u>are</u> ducks, but they look more like Woody Woodpecker, with long narrow bills and usually crests on their heads. Their bills have serrations for grasping and holding prey. Expert swimmers, they are hunters, not dabblers, and feed mainly on fish which they pursue underwater.

Because of their diet, mergansers are not considered prime game. Although they may present a hunting challenge, their flesh is fishy-flavored and disappointing. More than one proud hunter has blamed the cook for the

male-crest raised   female
Hooded Merganser

taste of his prize duck. It's not the sauce — it's the bird!

"fishing" female Hooded Merganser

J WIESSINGER

Looking or Listening?

An American Robin hops along the lawn, stops, tilts its head and then grabs a worm. Ever wonder how it found that worm?

American Robin

The robin is <u>looking</u> for the tips of worms at the entrance to their burrows. Most birds, like the robin, have eyes at the sides of their heads, giving them a "wide angle view" of the world. For a good close-up view, however, they often direct only one eye at their food. Since they can't roll their eyes as we do, they simply tilt the head in that direction and may appear to be listening, rather than looking, for food.

Headlines

What do these animals have in common?

Blackstripe Topminnow

Ornate Chorus Frog

The simplest way to avoid being eaten is to "disappear." But round, dark, shiny eyes can make an easy target for predators even when the rest of the body is well hidden.

Many animals make up for this with stripes or head patterns which continue through the eye and help to hide it. It isn't easy to hide the shine, but if the eye is just part of a larger dark pattern, the shape and shine are much harder to see. And a predator can't catch what it doesn't see!

Baby Western Painted Turtle

Song Sparrow

Look Again

Whenever you walk in the woods, you can be sure that many pairs of unseen eyes are watching you. How do their owners stay hidden? One way is through camouflage. Camouflage can take many forms, from matching the main background color to reducing telltale shadows to posing in imitation of a dead branch.

American Woodcock

The American Woodcock uses cryptic (KRIP-tik) coloration to blend with its background of dead leaves. Its busy pattern of light and dark browns is nearly indistinguishable from its surroundings—as long as the bird holds still! (Look again— what else do you see?)

Blending is Better

Camouflage is important to most animals. Predators need to stalk prey without being seen, while prey need to escape detection. Several means of camouflage can reduce visibility but one of the most common is **COUNTERSHADING**.

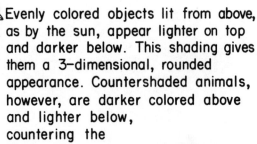

Evenly colored objects lit from above, as by the sun, appear lighter on top and darker below. This shading gives them a 3-dimensional, rounded appearance. Countershaded animals, however, are darker colored above and lighter below, countering the shading effect. By eliminating shading, an animal appears flatter, and blends into its surroundings.

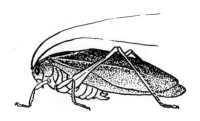

Turkey On Display

From the Thanksgiving centerpieces we usually see, it's easy to think that all Wild Turkeys look like the puffed up one shown here. This is a courtship posture, however, used by male turkeys to attract the females in the spring.

typical alert posture

courtship posture

WILD TURKEY

JWIESSINGER

The Wild Turkey's worst enemy is probably the mingling of semi-domesticated birds with the wild populations. Unlike their domestic relatives, Wild Turkeys are alert and extremely wary; mixed offspring decrease the survival success of the overall population.

As you prepare your Thanksgiving bird, enjoy your centerpiece for what it really is: a bit of SPRING in November!

Serious Business

Birdsongs may sound to us like joyful, carefree praise to spring, but for the singing males they are serious business.

These "happy" songs actually have two important messages: to proclaim "ownership" of a certain area, and to attract a mate. A male's song warns away other males by announcing the singer's residence on a "territory" or suitable nesting and feeding area. To a female, the song says just the opposite: it is the male's way of saying he is looking for a mate.

House Wren

44

Early Bird

Just when winter is at its worst, the Great Horned Owl begins to call in the woods, signalling its nesting season! Even February is not too bleak a month for it to begin laying eggs, usually in an abandoned hawk, heron, or crow nest.

Incubating Great Horned Owl

Why so early? Its eggs require a full month of incubation. With an early start, the owl chicks hatch when exposed ground and increasing rodent populations make hunting easier for their parents. Then the young have a long summer season in which to learn to hunt for themselves.

Great Horned Owl chick

45

Over Easy

An incubating bird must do more than just keep its eggs warm. Birds turn and rearrange their eggs periodically until the chicks hatch. Egg turning prevents the developing embryo's membranes from sticking to the inside of the egg shell. It also probably helps keep all of the eggs at a fairly even temperature. Each time the egg is turned, the embryo inside rotates to the top, where it gets maximum heat from its parent.

Pied-billed Grebe

Egg turning seems like a very minor bird behavior. But if artificial incubators like those on poultry farms don't rotate their eggs regularly, only a few eggs hatch.

Jail Break

Everyone knows that birds don't have teeth! Or do they?

Birds don't have true teeth, but ready-to-hatch babies have a special growth on the tip of their upper bills which helps them hatch. This "egg tooth" is a horny tubercle which helps to cut through the eggshell. A special hatching muscle at the back of the neck provides the power to use the egg tooth during the critical hatching period.

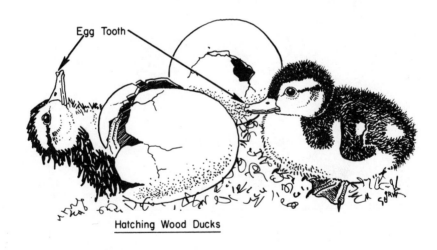

Egg Tooth

Hatching Wood Ducks

Once the young bird breaks out of its "jail," the egg tooth and hatching muscle are no longer needed. The tooth soon drops off and the muscle shrinks in size.

Take Your Pick

A robin's hatchling is bare, blind, floppy, and helpless — completely dependent on its parents. Although Killdeer and robins are about the same size, a Killdeer's egg is much larger, and its chick hatches feathered, bright-eyed, and ready to run and find its own food. A better way? It depends.

day-old
American Robin

Helpless "altricial" (al-TRISH-al) young hatch early, grow very quickly, and leave the nest soon. The lively "precocial" (pre-CO-shal) young have a longer incubation, mature more slowly and stay with their parents longer. With some variations, all birds succeed with one of these two ways of raising their young.

day-old
Killdeer

Foster Care

All across North America every year, female cowbirds lay their eggs in the nests of other species and leave them to be raised by foster parents. Neither the Bronzed nor Brown-headed Cowbird raises its own young.

baby Brown-headed Cowbird in Yellow Warbler nest

The cowbird's incubation is usually shorter than its hosts and its chicks are large and grow very quickly. The cowbird young (usually one per nest) often gets the lion's share of food and one or more of the rightful young may starve or be forced from the nest. Some birds refuse to incubate cowbird eggs but many species care for the foundling as if it were their own.

adult Brown-headed Cowbird
15-20 cm (6-8")

49

That's Hard To Swallow!

HOW DOES A PARENT BIRD ENSURE THAT ALL ITS BABIES GET THEIR FULL SHARE OF FOOD?

The babies do it themselves! After a young bird swallows food, its swallowing reflex stops functioning for a few moments. If a second bit of food is placed too soon in a gaping mouth, the food does not disappear. The parent sees it, removes it, and puts it in another mouth. This makes it possible to provide an equal distribution of food. Share and share alike!

Yellow-rumped Warbler

Disposable Diapers

Why isn't a bird's nest badly soiled by the time the young leave?

Nest sanitation is very important if the young are to remain healthy. Most songbirds and woodpeckers have a clever way to ensure that their nests stay clean and odor-free.

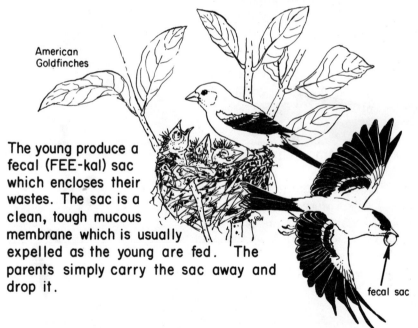

American Goldfinches

The young produce a fecal (FEE-kal) sac which encloses their wastes. The sac is a clean, tough mucous membrane which is usually expelled as the young are fed. The parents simply carry the sac away and drop it.

fecal sac

There's more than one way to make a disposable diaper!

Bird vs. Bonnet

In the early 1900's, egrets
were almost extinct. During
the breeding season, egrets
grow fancy white plumes.
But eighty years ago, plume
hunters could get up to $32 an
ounce for those lovely feathers!
Ladies' hats flourished, and egrets
nearly disappeared.

Snowy Egret

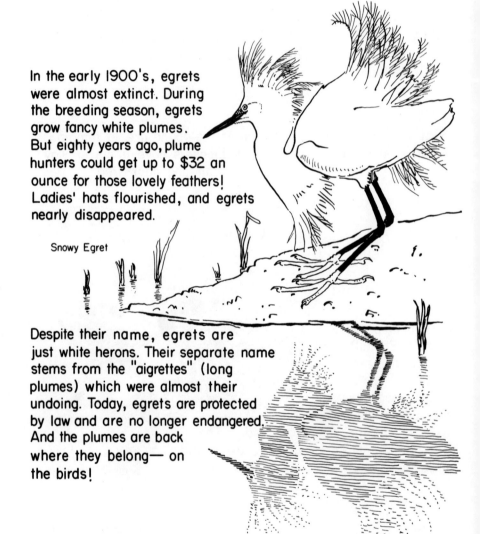

Despite their name, egrets are
just white herons. Their separate name
stems from the "aigrettes" (long
plumes) which were almost their
undoing. Today, egrets are protected
by law and are no longer endangered.
And the plumes are back
where they belong— on
the birds!

Alien Invasion

It has been just over a century since the first Starlings arrived in New York City from Europe. Yet in that time, they have usurped the nesting cavities of native hole-nesting birds from the Atlantic to the Pacific. Often it takes an "outsider" to take full advantage of available resources. And the Starling has done it!

Starling in winter

Starling in summer

Starlings (often called blackbirds) are attractive birds— glossy black with yellow bills in summer, white-spotted with dark bills in winter. But their exploding population and their enormous, raucous winter congregations have earned them one of the worst reputations in the bird world.

To the Rescue?

Each year thousands of "abandonded" baby cottontails are doomed when well-meaning people bring them home. Actually, the mother is probably just a few feet away. She stays away from the babies during daylight but is nearby to watch for predators, often luring them away from her young.

Cottontail

American Robin

"Orphaned" fledgling birds are usually fine, too, with a parent feeding them at intervals. It is <u>extremely</u> hard to provide proper care and food for adopted wild babies. At best, they are often stunted and ill-equipped for survival; at worst, they die slowly of malnutrition. Do them a favor. Let them be!

Flying Cigars

Not all animals have suffered from man's expansion. Before European settlers arrived here, Chimney Swifts relied on hollow trees for nest sites. Today, they prefer chimneys and silos to their traditional homes. As nesting sites have increased, so have swifts.

The nest is glued to a vertical surface with special saliva (like that used in Chinese "bird's nest soup"). Swifts, too, cling vertically with their small but strong feet. Their fat, sleek, "legless" look in the air has earned them the nickname "FLYING CIGARS."

Typical Chimney Swift nest glued to vertical chimney wall.

Helping the Horde

The Evening Grosbeak "horde" may descend on your bird feeder one winter and not at all the next. Here's why.

Evening Grosbeaks

Evening Grosbeaks are most common in Canada; 150 years ago they were unknown in the eastern U.S. But when their winter food supply — evergreen and maple seeds — is poor they must move southward for food. Partly because of help from bird feeders, their numbers and range have greatly increased in recent decades. In some winters they even push deep into the southeastern states — hungry but colorful visitors from the North.

O Christmas Tree

Evergreen trees do more than just add beauty to the winter holidays. They provide excellent protection for many animals from the wind, the cold, and the rain. Nighttime is particularly difficult for small birds during cold or wet winter weather. The evergreen branches — especially snow-covered ones — provide insulated shelter to keep birds alive through a long winter's night.

Sleeping
Sparrow

If you have even a small area of dense evergreen trees or shrubs near your home, it may be serving as a vital nighttime roost.

Sharing

Why is there so much concern
about the destruction of South
American rain forests? Can
cutting down trees so far away
really affect us?

Northern Oriole

Yes! In many ways, large and small.
One of the most obvious effects is
right outside our door. Each year
large numbers of our birds— flycatchers,
warblers, and orioles among them — winter in South
America. They rely on the habitats there for food and
shelter until they return in the spring.
The most bountiful habitat here is no
good to a bird that died down there.
If we want to protect "our" birds, we
must remember that they are also "theirs."

A Success Story?

Whooping Cranes have been saved from extinction— <u>for</u> <u>now</u>.

In 1941 there were only 15 Whooping Cranes left in the wild! Through habitat preservation, public education and lots of luck, these impressive birds were salvaged. Today there are about 140 wild birds but their future is still very uncertain.

Many other species have also had their numbers critically reduced. Some may never recover; others may. But whenever an organism's population drops to a very low level— even if extinction is averted— much of its diversity is lost forever. Suppose we had to rebuild the human population from 15 individuals. Which 15 would you pick? What would we lose?

Whooping Crane

Why Care?

Red Wolf

An "endangered species" is any organism which will probably become extinct if the current threats to its survival are not changed. Unfortunately, most of these threats are a result of human-caused environmental changes.

Peregrine Falcon

Desert Chub

Black Toad

Why does it matter? Many scientists would say we are performing worldwide experiments, without knowing the possible outcomes and without any known way of backing up when we make a serious mistake. All of life is a tangled web of interdependent species. Every species lost to human "tinkering" may sever a tiny thread in our own safety net. How many threads dare we break? Who wants to find out?

California Condor

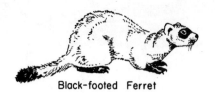

Black-footed Ferret

INDEX

abandoned birds, 54
aigrettes, 52
altricial young, 48
alula, 26
American Goldfinch, 51
American Robin
  abandoned baby, 54
  as partial migrant, 33
  asleep on perch, 20
  looking for food, 39
  young, 48
American Woodcock, 41
animal definition, 7

baby birds
  altricial, 48
  American Goldfinch, 51
  American Robin, 48, 54
  American Woodcock, 41
  Brown-headed Cowbird, 49
  ducks, 47
  Great Horned Owl, 45
  precocial, 48
  Yellow warbler, 49
  Yellow-rumped Warbler, 50
Baltimore Oriole. *See* Northern
  Oriole

Barn owl, 35
Barn Swallow, 21
beak. *See* bill
beneficial species, 60
bill
  adaptations of, 37
  of mergansers, 38
bird feeder, 56
blackbirds
  Bronzed Cowbird, 49
  Brown-headed Cowbird, 49
  Red-winged Blackbird, 14
  Starling, 53
blood circulation, 19
Bronzed Cowbird, 49
Brown-headed Cowbird, 49

California Condor, 60
call of Killdeer, 15
camouflage
  and countershading, 42
  and cryptic coloration, 41
  in domestic animals, 10
  of eye, 40
Canada Goose, 32
Cardinal, 22
chicks. *See* baby birds

Chimney Swift, 55
Chipping Sparrow, 12
Condor, California, 60
countershading, 42
courtship postures. *See* display
     postures
Cowbird
   Bronzed, 49
   Brown-headed, 49
Crane
   Sandhill, 11
   Whooping, 59
cryptic coloration. *See* camouflage

dish face, 35
display postures
   of Red-winged Blackbird, 14
   of Snowy Egret, 52
   of Wild Turkey, 43
Downy Woodpecker, 13
duck bill, 37
Duck
   domestic, 10
   Mallard, 10, 19, 29
   Merganser, 38
   Redhead, 17
   Wood, 47
Dunlin. *See* shorebirds

egg
   altricial or precocial, 48
   care of, 46
   hatching from, 47
egg tooth, 47
Egret
   Great, 8
   Snowy, 52
endangered species
   California Condor, 60
   Peregrine Falcon, 60
   Snowy Egret, 52
   Whooping Crane, 59
epaulet, 14
Evening Grosbeak, 56
extinction
   and reasons for concern, 60
   of egrets, 52
   of Whooping Crane, 59

eye (*see also* vision)
   camouflage of, 40
eyelid, 21

Falcon, Peregrine, 60
feathers
   aigrettes, 52
   alula, 26
   color of, 24
   epaulets, 14
   insulation, 17, 18, 33
   oiling, 17
   plumes, 52
   serrations on, 36
   silent flight, 36
   unique to birds, 8
fecal sac, 51
feeder birds, 12, 56
feet
   freezing of, 19
   as "snowshoes," 28
Finches
   American Goldfinch, 51
   bills of, 37
   Cardinals, 22
   Evening Grosbeake, 56
flight
   alula and, 26
   posture during, 11
   nictitating membrane during, 21
   speed of, 25
   "V" formation, 32
flycatchers, 58
food
   for migration, 30
   for young, 49, 50
   searching for, 13, 34, 38, 39, 45
formation flying. *See* flight

Goose, Canada, 32
goggles, 21
gorget, 23
Great Horned Owl
   chick, 45
   nesting, 45
   niche of, 9
Grebe, Pied-billed, 46
Grosbeaks, Evening, 56
Grouse, Ruffed, 28

62

habitat
 destruction of, 58
 migration to new, 29
 preservation of, 59
 suitability of, 14
hatching, 46, 47
Hawk
 bill of, 37
 Red-shouldered, 26
 Red-tailed, 9
hearing
 in owls, 35, 36
 in robins, 39
helpful to humans. *See* Beneficial
  species
Heron
 bill of, 37
 Great Blue, 11
 Great Egret, 8
 Snowy Egret, 52
House Wren, 44
Hummingbird, Ruby-throated
 bill of, 37
 gorget, 23

incubation
 altricial *vs.* precocial, 48
 of cowbird, 49
 of Pied-billed Grebe, 46
 of owl, 45
introduced species, 53

Killdeer
 habitat of, 15
 young, 48
Mallard
 domestic *vs.* wild, 10
 feet, 19
 migration of, 29
merganser, 38
migration, 58
 navigation during, 31
 partial, 33
 preparation for, 30
 reasons for, 29, 56
 to South America, 58
 "V" formation during, 32

muscles
 and goosebumps, 18
 and perching, 20
 dark *vs* light, 27
Myrtle Warbler. *See* Yellow-
  rumped Warbler

nest
 of Chimney Swift, 55
 of Great-horned Owl, 45
 of Killdeer, 15
 of Pied-billed Grebe, 46
 of Yellow Warbler, 49
 of Yellow-rumped Warbler, 50
 sanitation of, 51
niche, 9
nictitating membrane, 21
Northern Oriole, 30, 58
Nuthatch, White-breasted, 13

Oriole. *See* Northern Oriole
orphaned birds, 54
Owl
 Barn, 35
 chick, 45
 Great-horned, 9, 45
 Screech, 36

perching, 20
Peregrine Falcon, 25, 60
Pheasant, Ring-necked, 27
Pied-billed Grebe, 46
plover. *See* Killdeer
precocial young, 41, 47, 48
preen gland, 17
preening, 17

Redhead Duck, 17
Ring-necked Pheasant, 27
Red-tailed Hawk, 9
Robin
 "abandoned" baby, 54
 as partial migrant, 33
 asleep on perch, 20
 baby, 48
 looking for food, 39
Ruby-throated Hummingbird, 23
Ruffed Grouse, 28

sandpiper. *See* shorebirds
scrape. *See* nest
search image, 34
shelter, 57
shorebirds
  Dunlin, 25
  Killdeer, 15, 48
sleeping
  while perching, 20
  shelter for, 57
song
  reason for, 44
  structure for, 16
Song Sparrow, 12
  camouflaged eye in, 40
Sparrow
  Chipping, 12
  Song, 12, 40
  White-throated, 12
speed. *See* flight
Starling, 53
structural color
  of blue birds, 24
  of hummingbirds' gorget, 23
Swallow, Barn, 21
Swift
  Chimney, 55
  White-tailed, 25
syrinx, 16

tendons, 20
Thrush, Wood, 16
Turkey, 43

"V" formation, 32
vision
  color *vs*. black-and-white, 22
  night, 35,36
  Robins', 39

Warbler
  babies, 49, 50
  bill of, 37
  food searching by, 34
  wintering of, 58
  Yellow, 49
  Yellow-rumped, 50

White-breasted Nuthatch, 13
White-tailed Swift, 25
White-throated Sparrow, 12
Whooping Crane, 59
winter 33
  nesting in, 45
  travel in, 28
Wood Duck, 47
Wood Thrush, 16
Woodcock, American, 41
Woodpecker
  Downy, 13
  bill of, 37
Wren, House, 44

Yellow Warbler, 49
Yellow-rumped Warbler, 50